Scales

&

Broken Chords

Piano Grade 1

First published in the U.K. in 2015 by
The Ashton Book Company
9 Dairy Farm, Ashton Keynes,
Swindon, Wiltshire SN6 6NZ

ISBN-13: 978-1984052711
ISBN-10: 1984052713

Grade 1 scales and broken chords

This booklet contains all of the scales and broken chords that are set for the grade 1 piano exam.

In order to help with learning and memorising, the scales and broken chords are shown in 2 ways - as notes on a stave and also in picture form, with each picture showing the notes and fingering.

The scales and broken chords should be played neatly and with logical fingering. It is not necessary to use the exact fingering marked in this book, but it is recommended. The tone should be even and controlled.

The minimum speeds required for Grade 1 are:

scales: ♩ = 60

broken chords: 𝅗𝅥. = 46 (ie. ♩ = 138)

Please refer to the current syllabus for the exam board you are using to check the exact requirements.

MAJOR SCALES

2 Octaves

lead from your elbow iron out any bumps

C major scale - right hand

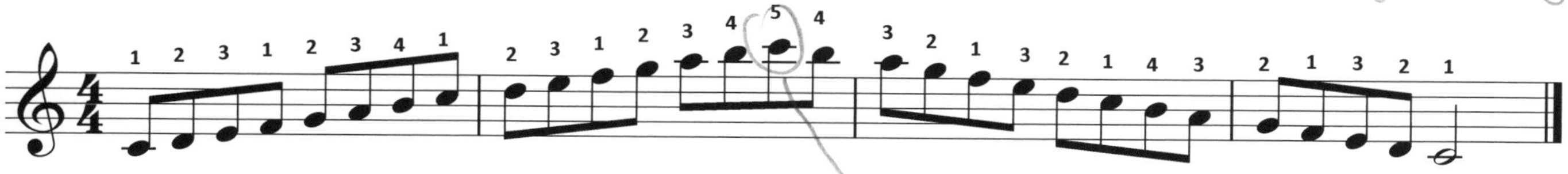

Right hand

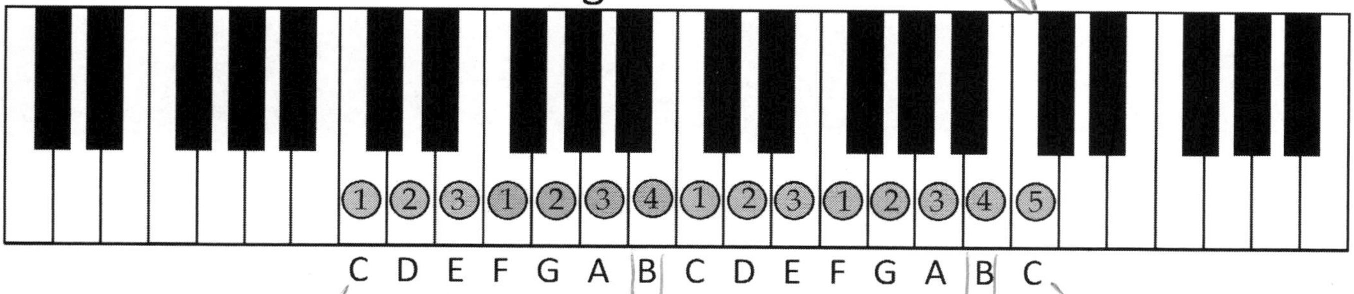

MIDDLE C

PUT 4TH FINGER ON B

5TH FINGER ON TOP NOTE!

C major scale - left hand

2Octaves (8ves)

OR

* Start

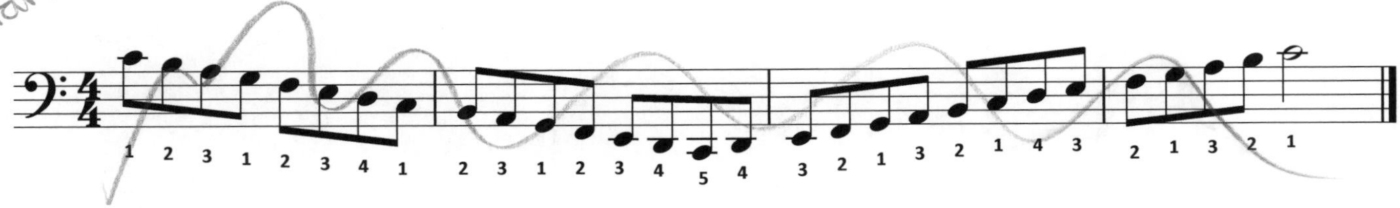

Left hand

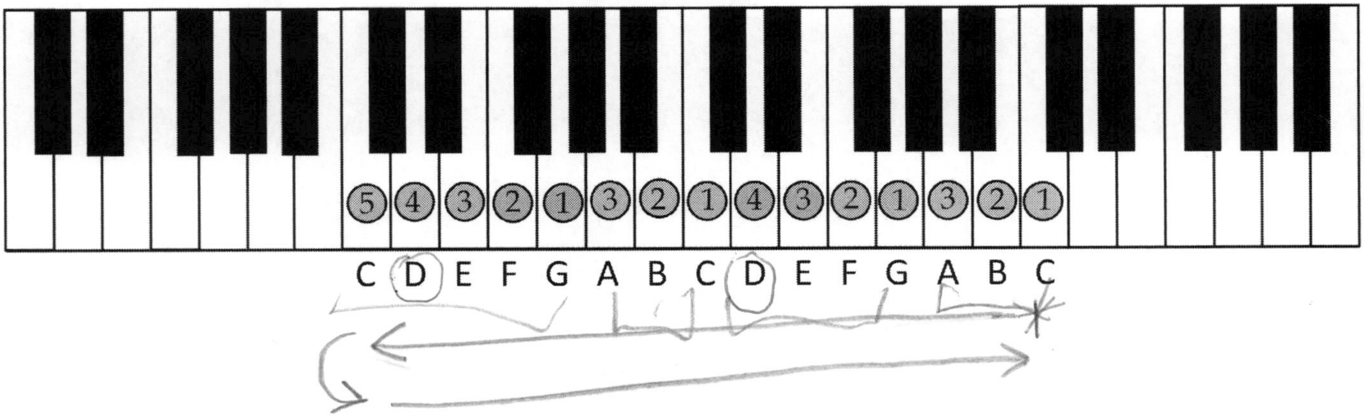

G major scale - right hand

Right hand

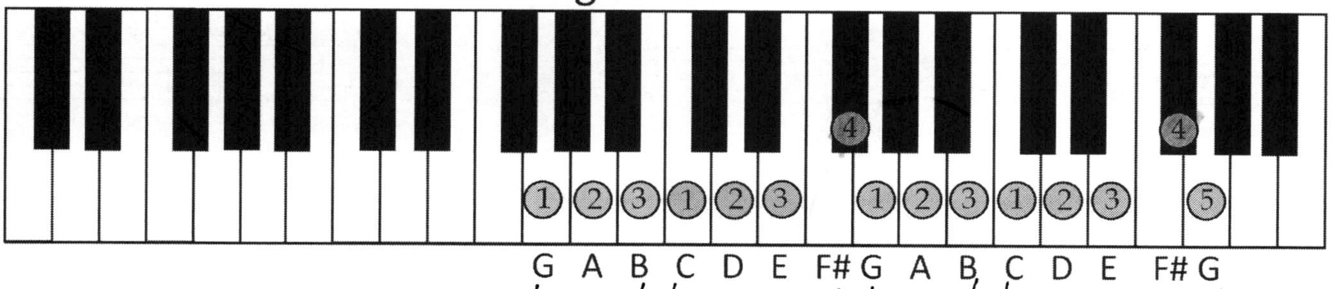

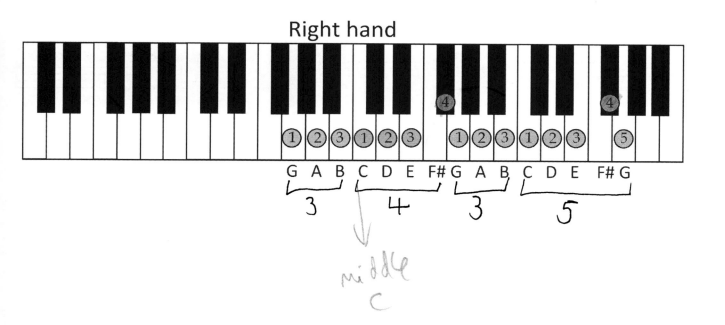

G major scale - left hand

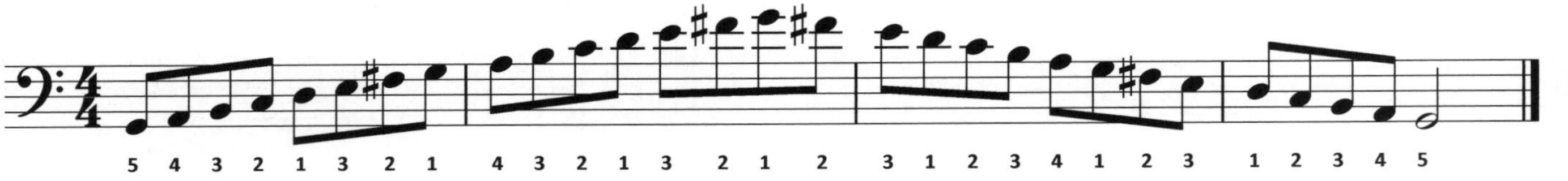

OR

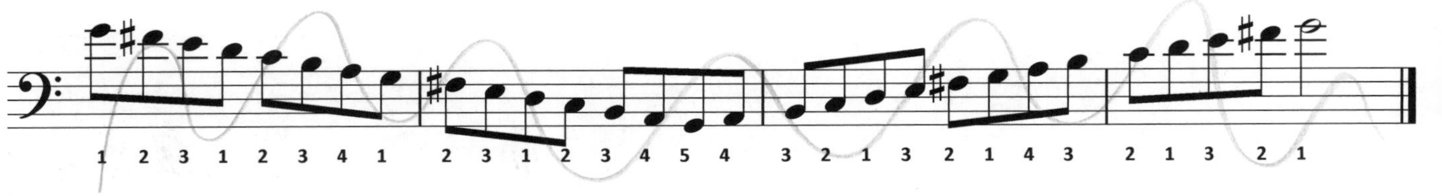

Left hand

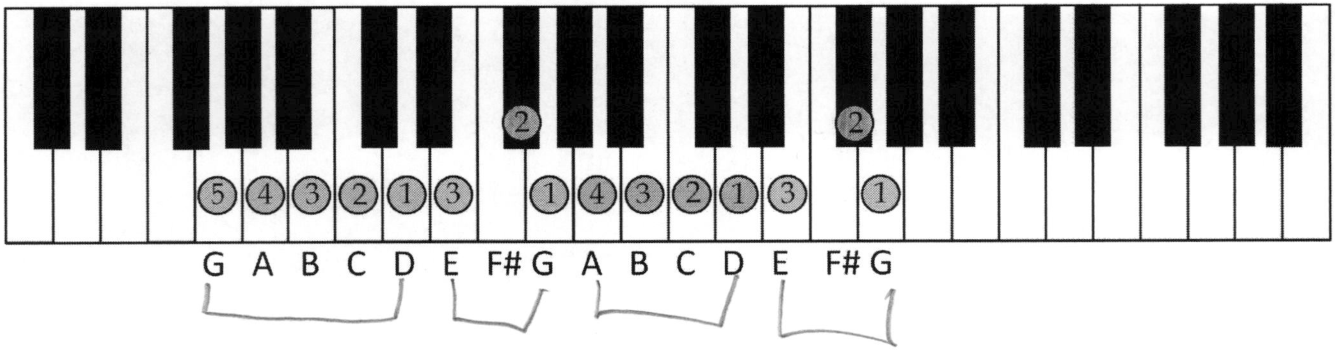

F major scale - right hand

Right hand

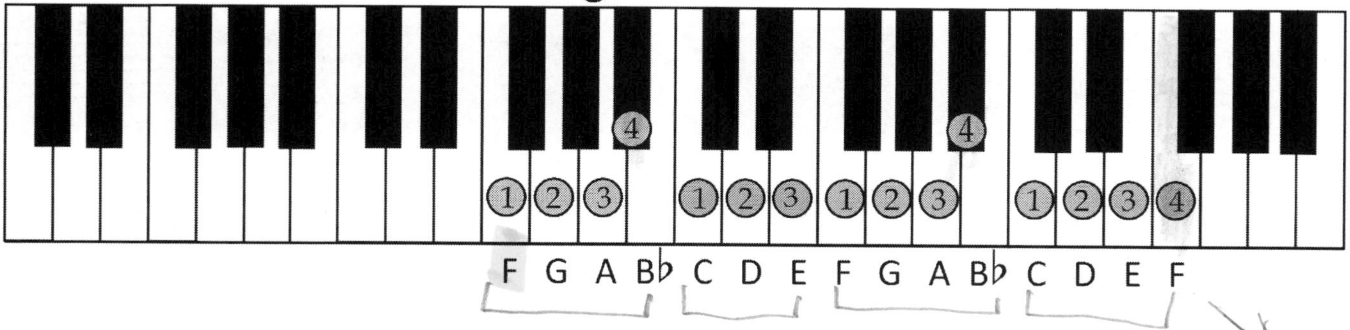

4 on ends

F major scale - left hand

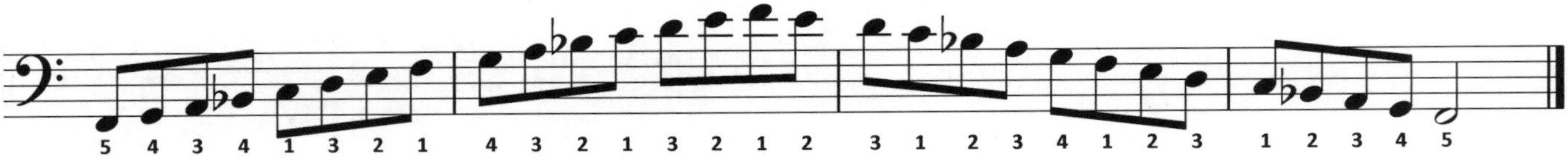

OR

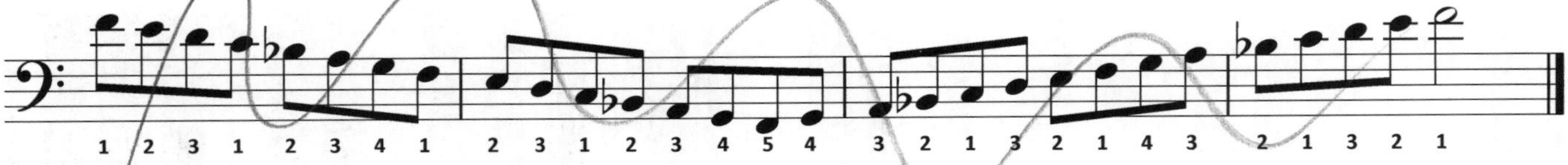

Left hand

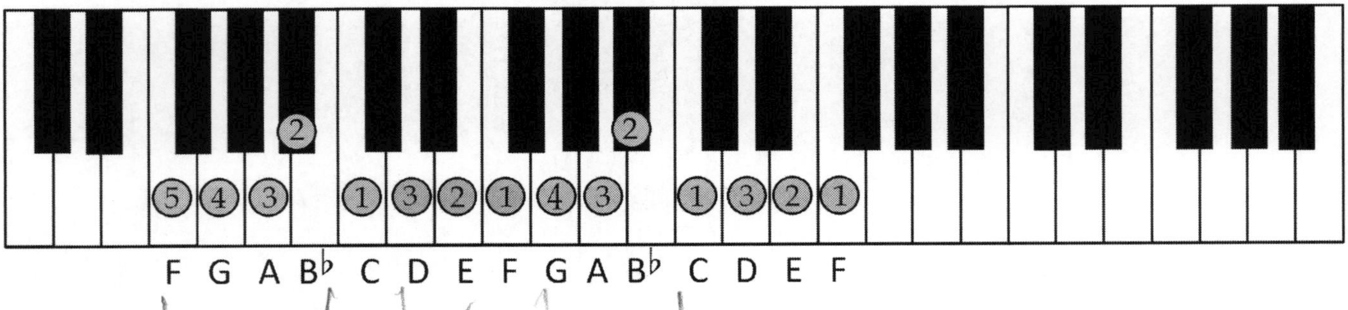

D major scale - right hand ✓

1 2 3 1 2 3 4 1 2 3 1 2 3 4 5 4 3 2 1 3 2 1 4 3 2 1 3 2 1

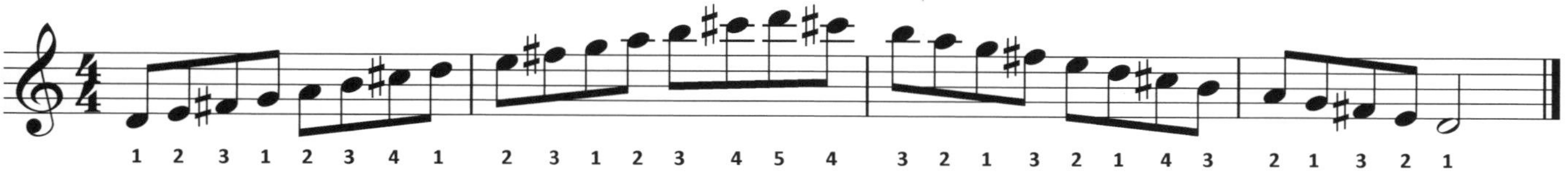

4th finger on C#s

Right hand

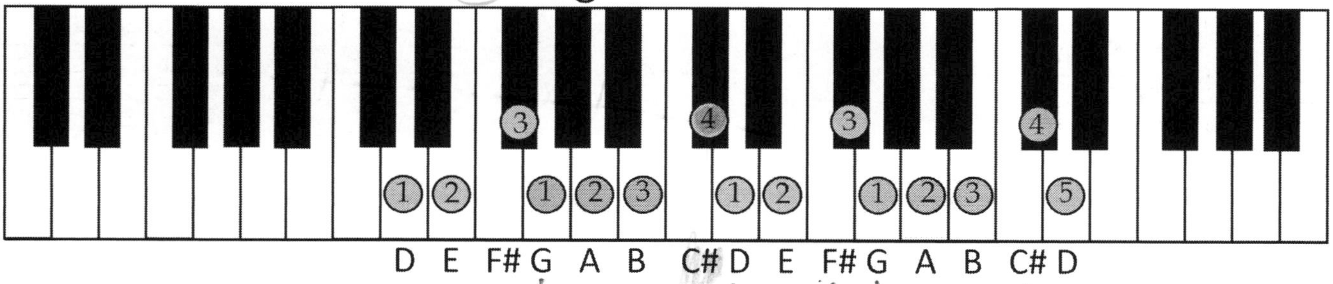

SHARP SIGN # #

more concentration

D major scale - left hand

OR

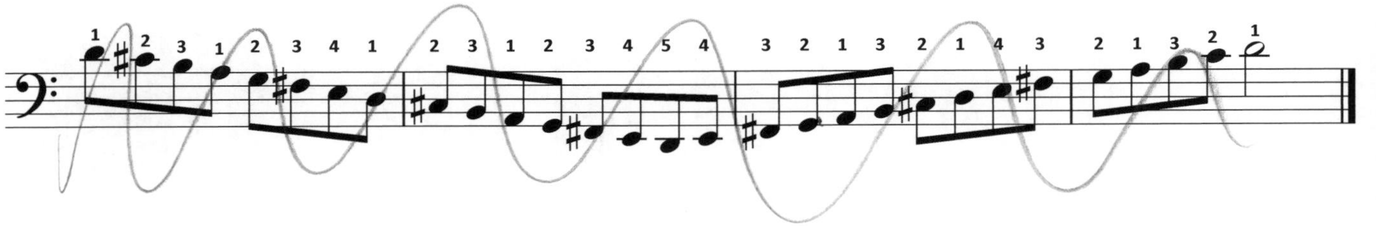

Left hand

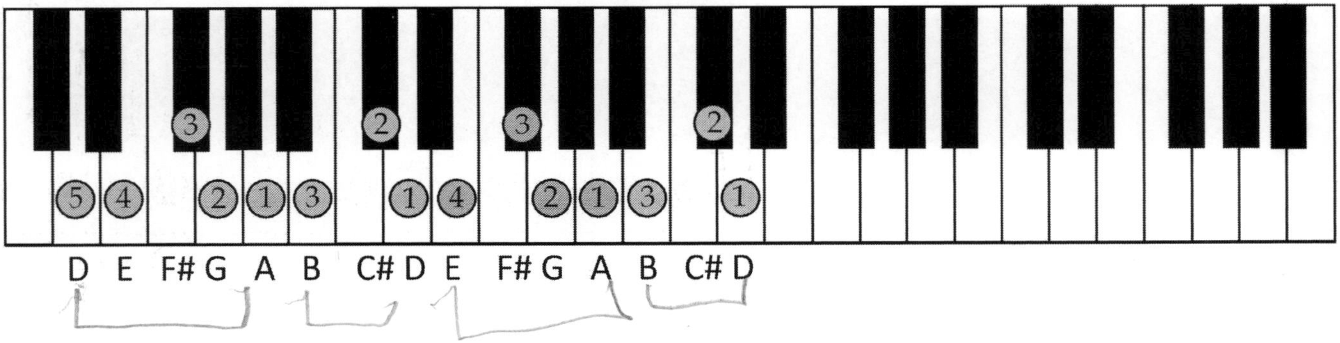

MINOR SCALES

A harmonic minor scale - right hand

Right hand

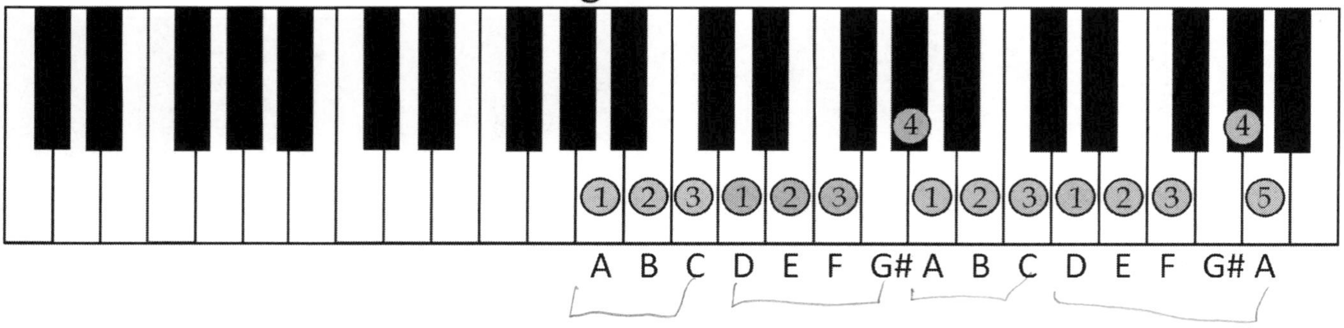

A harmonic minor scale - left hand

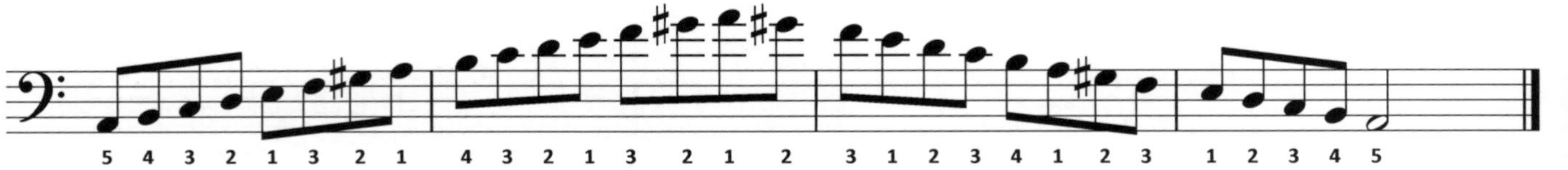

OR

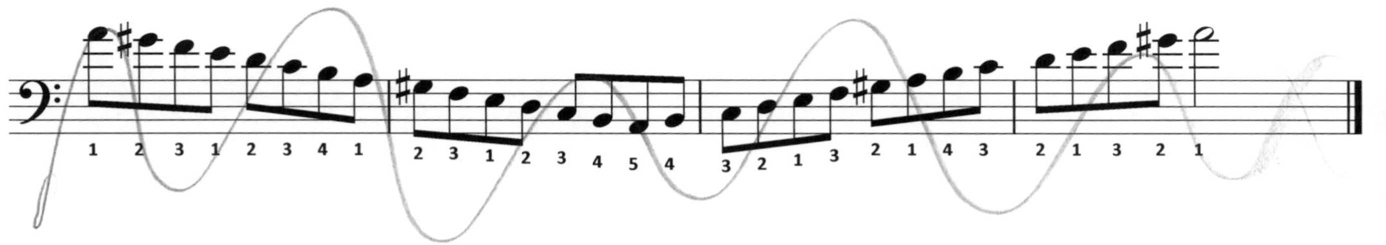

Left hand

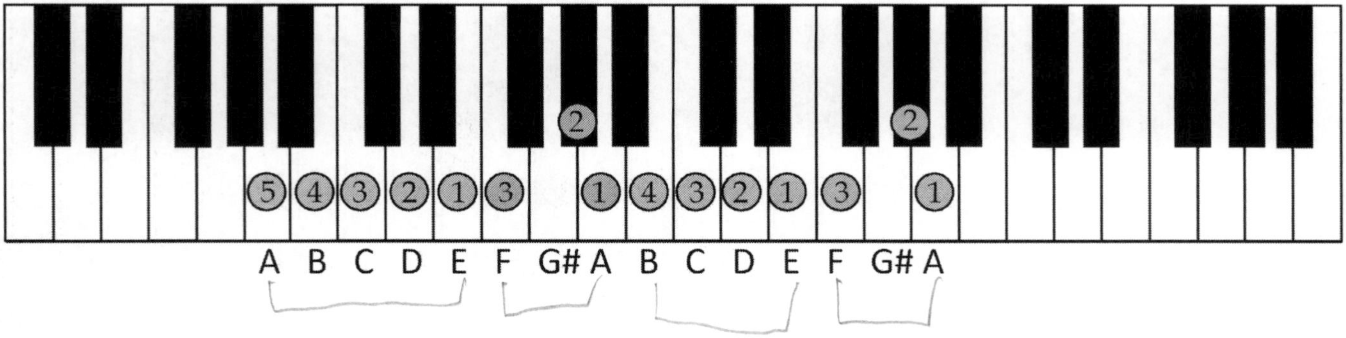

D harmonic minor scale - right hand

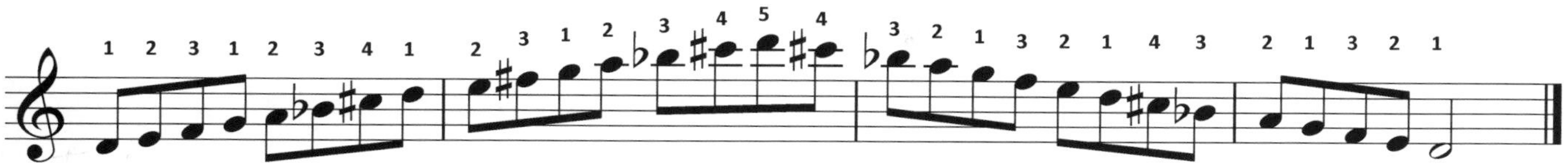

Right hand

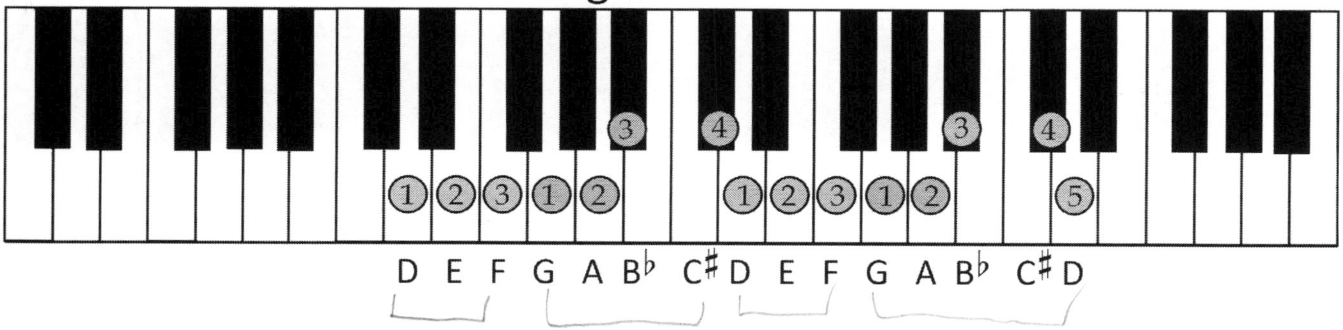

D harmonic minor scale - left hand

OR

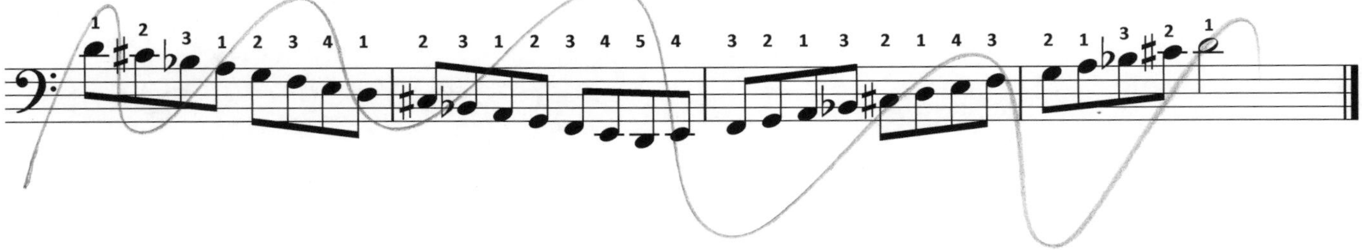

Left hand

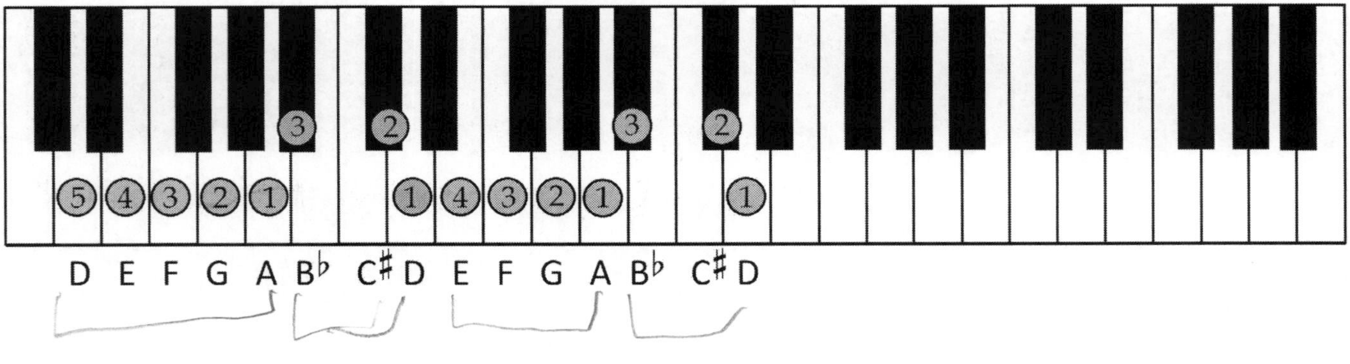

E harmonic minor scale - right hand

Right hand

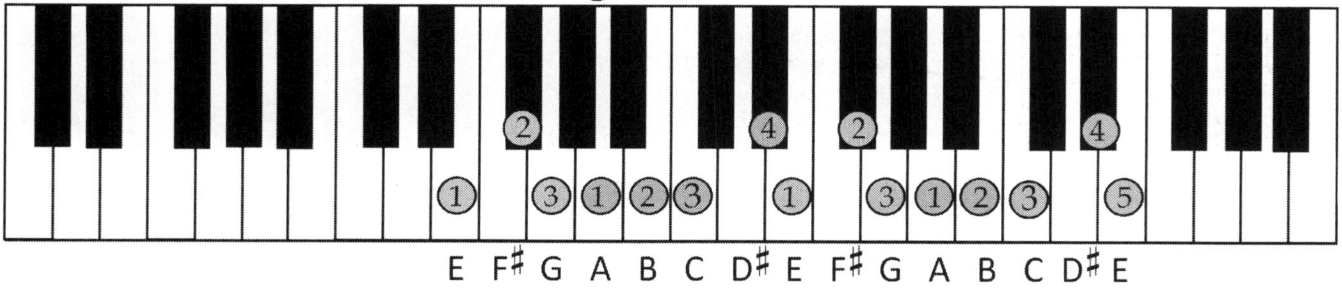

E harmonic minor scale - left hand

OR

Left hand

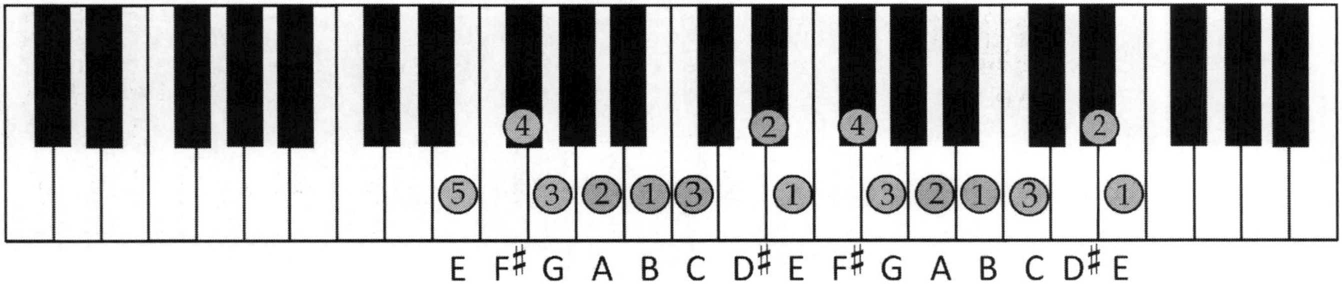

A melodic minor scale - right hand

Right hand - ascending

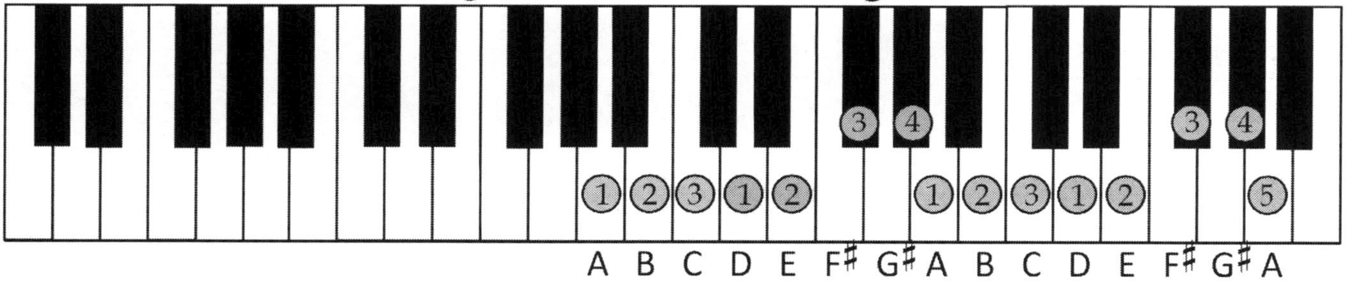

Right hand - descending

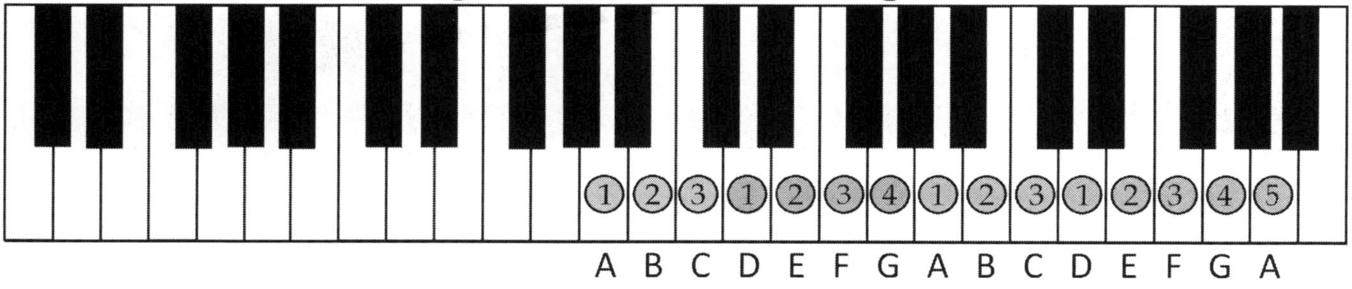

A melodic minor scale - left hand

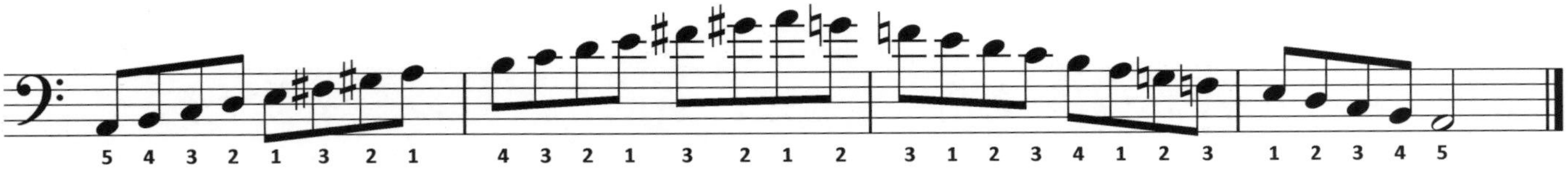

OR

Left hand - ascending

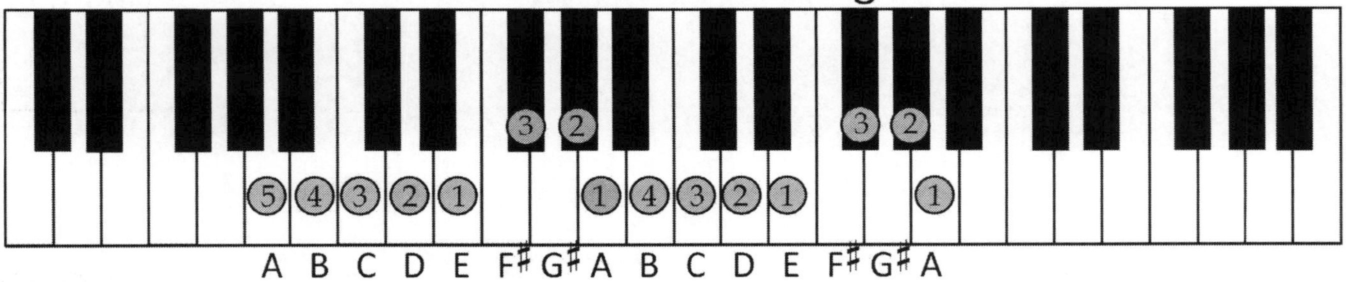

Left hand - descending

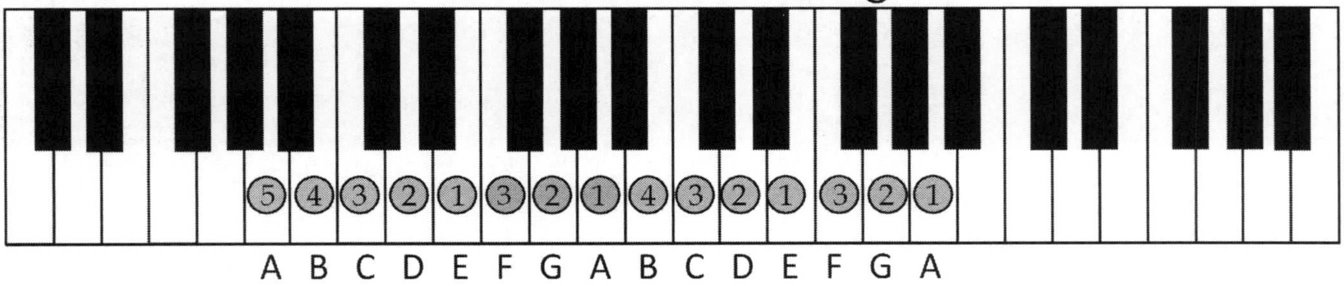

D melodic minor scale - right hand

Right hand - ascending

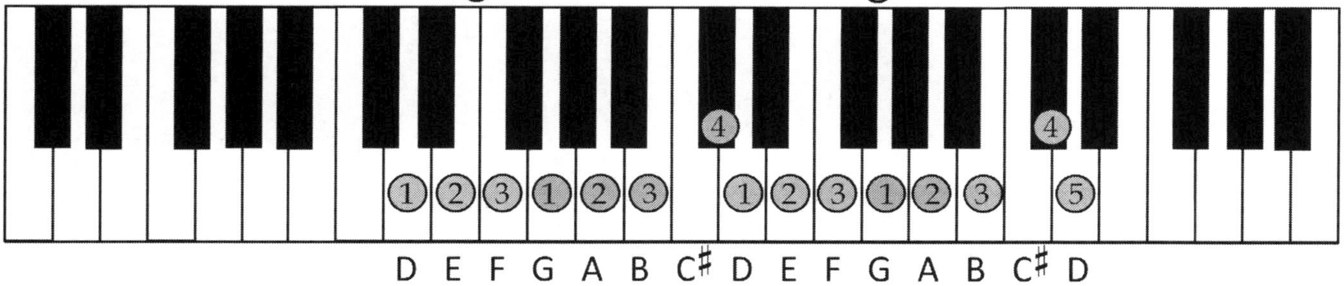

Right hand - descending

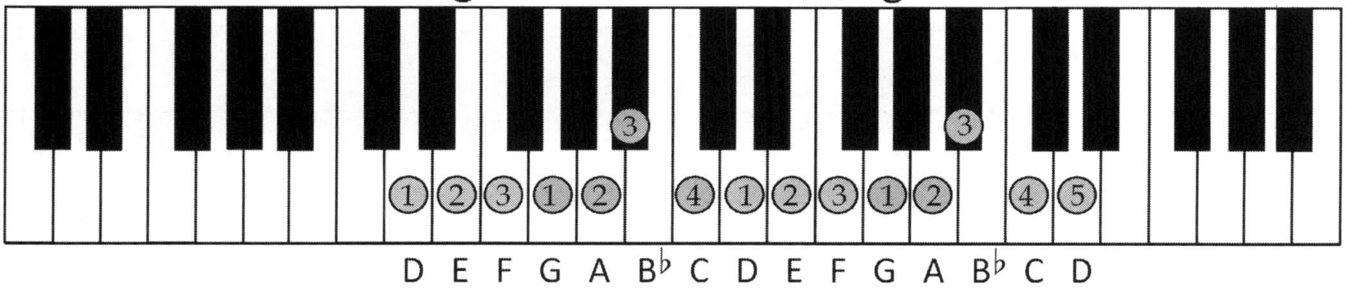

D melodic minor scale - left hand

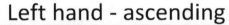

OR

Left hand - ascending

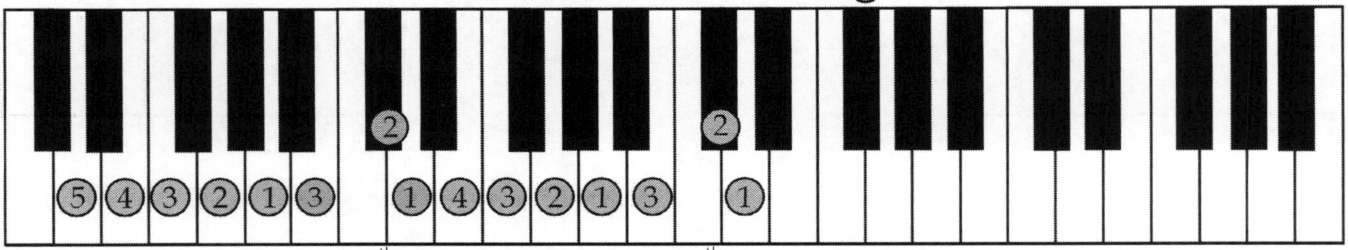

Left hand - descending

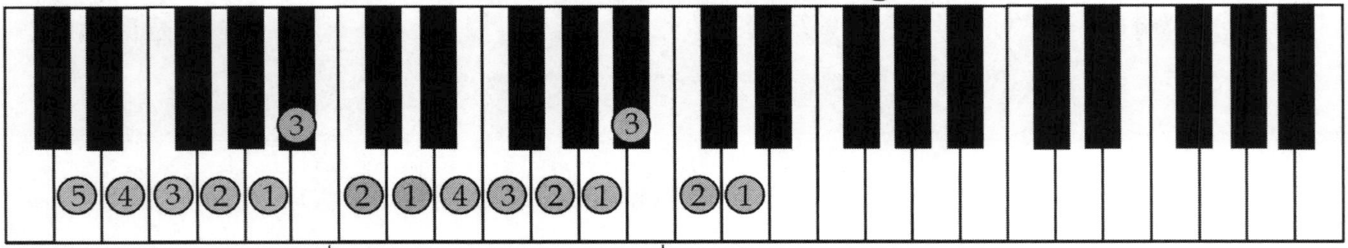

E melodic minor scale - right hand

Right hand ascending

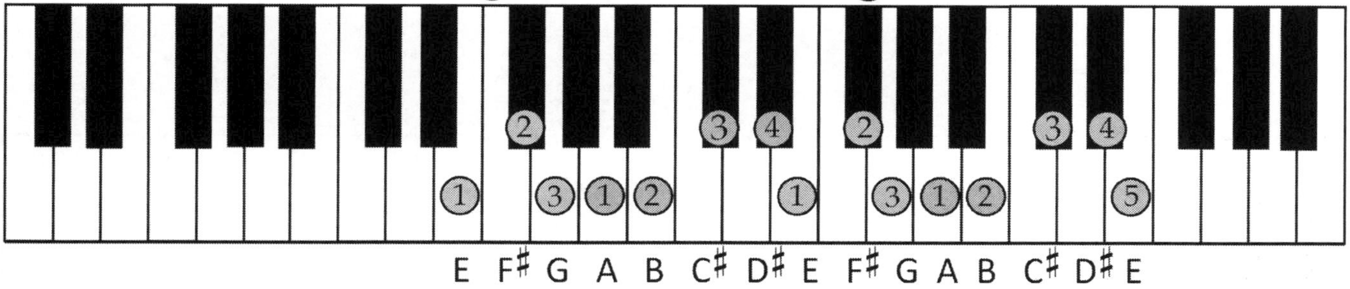

Right hand descending

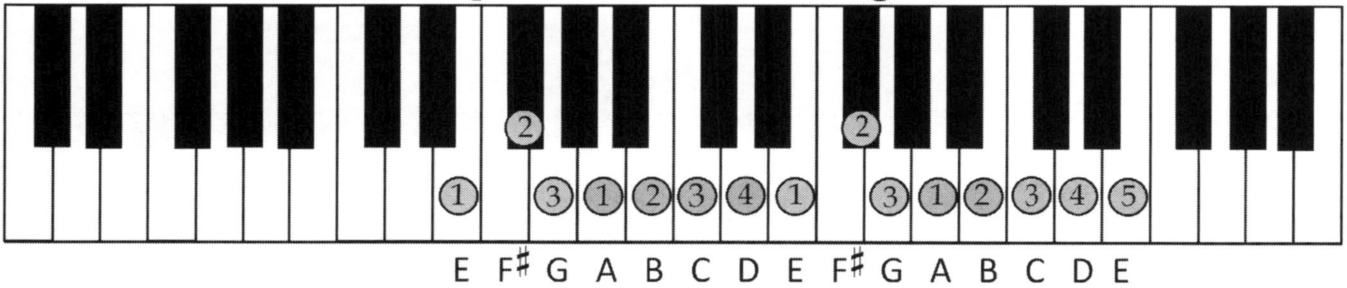

E melodic minor scale - left hand

OR

Left hand ascending

E F♯ G A B C♯ D♯ E F♯ G A B C♯ D♯ E

Left hand descending

E F♯ G A B C D E F♯ G A B C D E

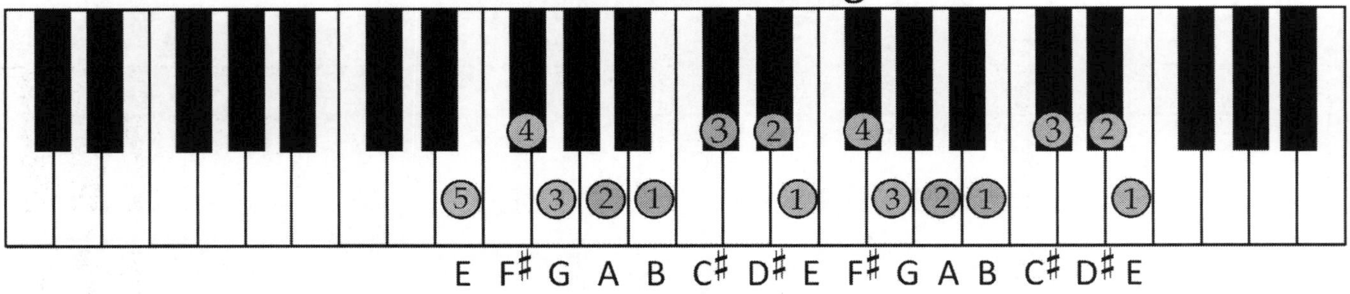

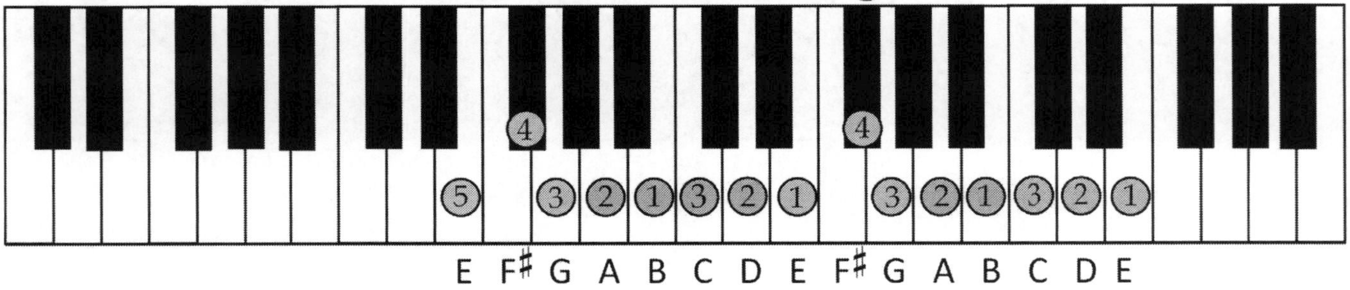

A natural minor scale - right hand

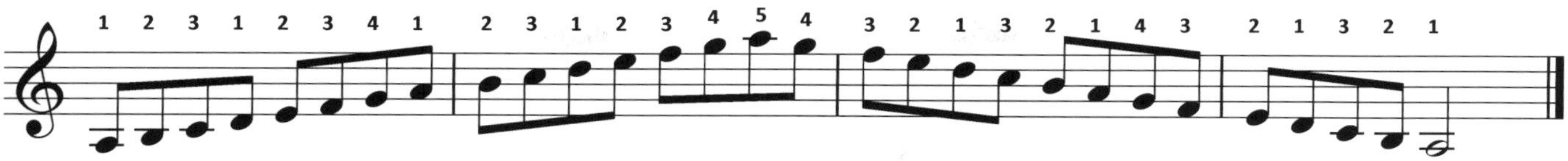

Right hand

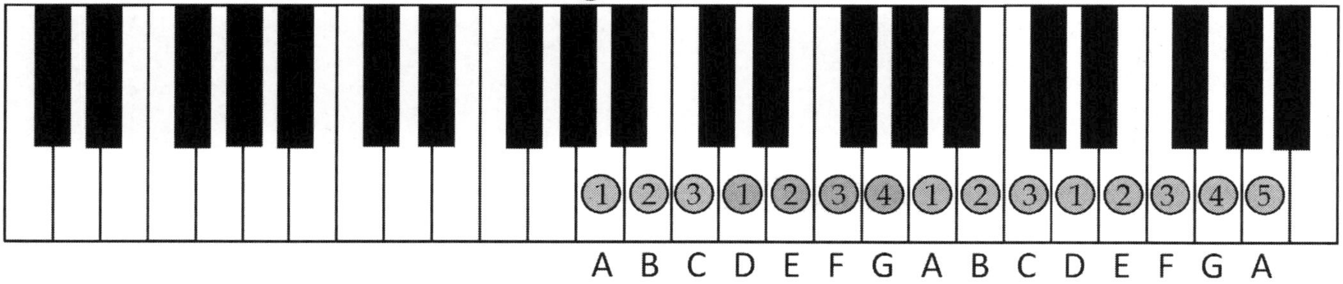

A natural minor scale - left hand

5 4 3 2 1 3 2 1 4 3 2 1 3 2 1 2 3 1 2 3 4 1 2 3 1 2 3 4 5

OR

1 2 3 1 2 3 4 1 2 3 1 2 3 4 5 4 3 2 1 3 2 1 4 3 2 1 3 2 1

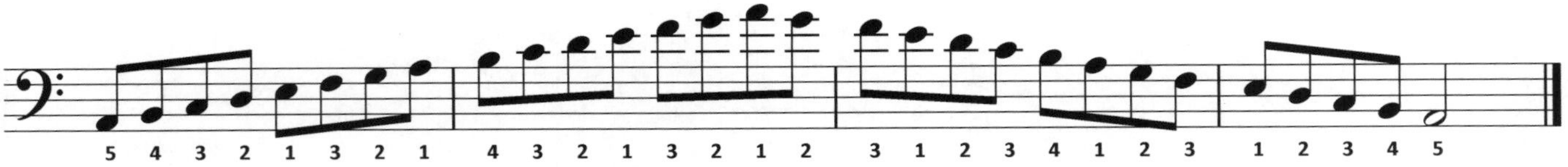

Left hand

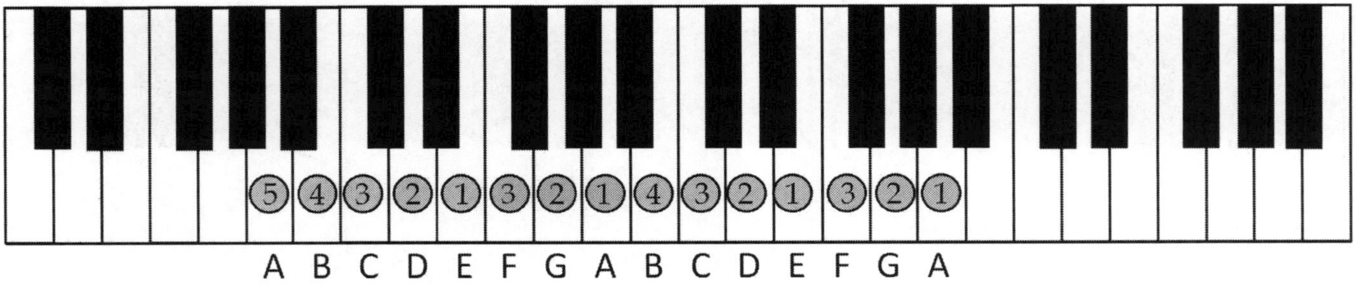

D natural minor scale - right hand

1 2 3 1 2 3 4 1 2 3 1 2 3 4 5 4 3 2 1 3 2 1 4 3 2 1 3 2 1

Right hand

D E F G A B♭ C D E F G A B♭ C D

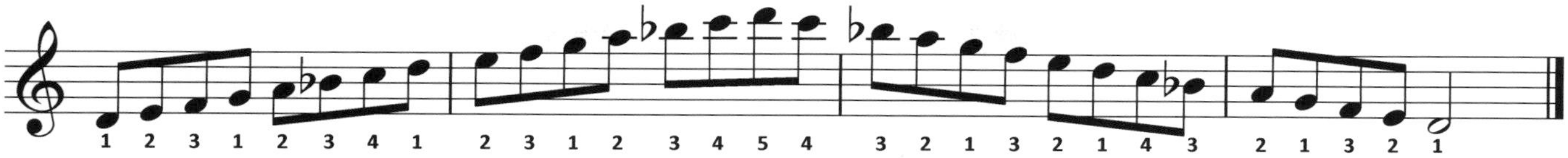

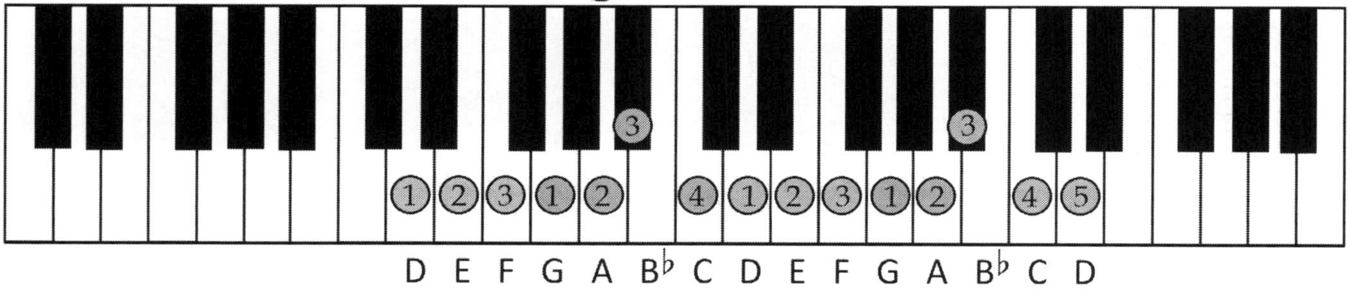

D natural minor scale - left hand

OR

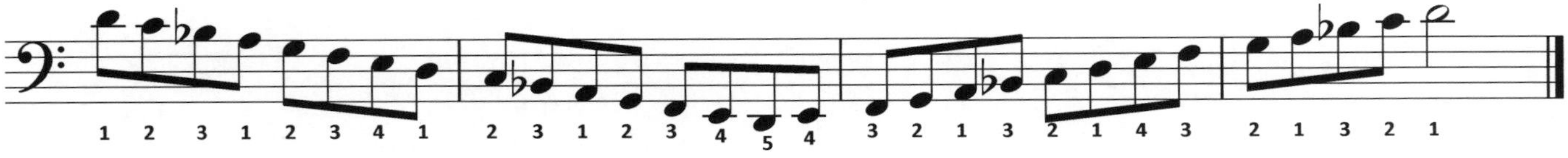

Left hand

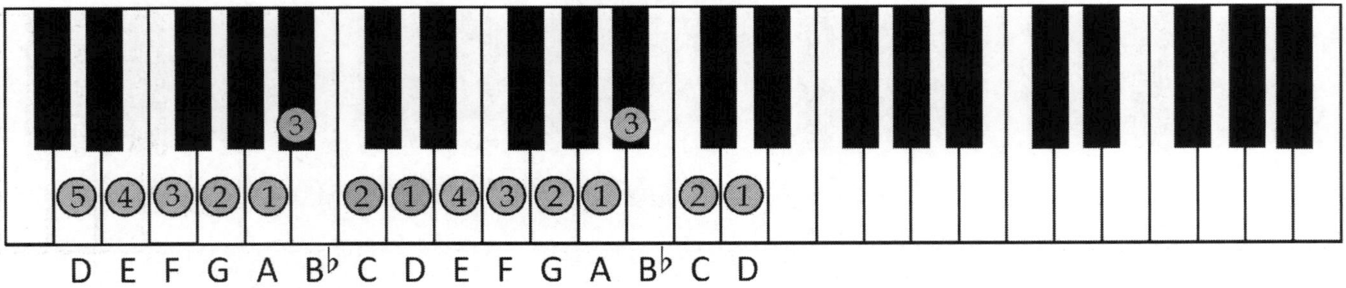

E natural minor scale - right hand

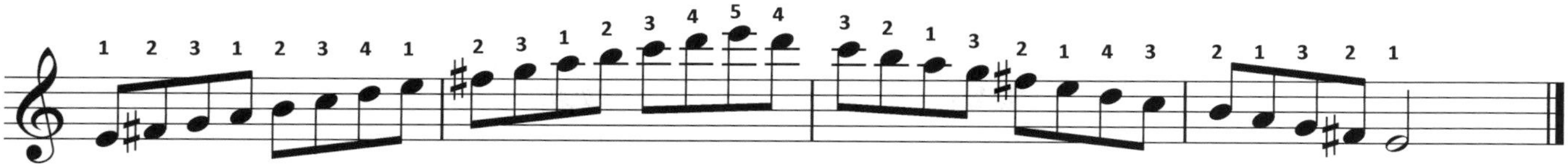

Right hand

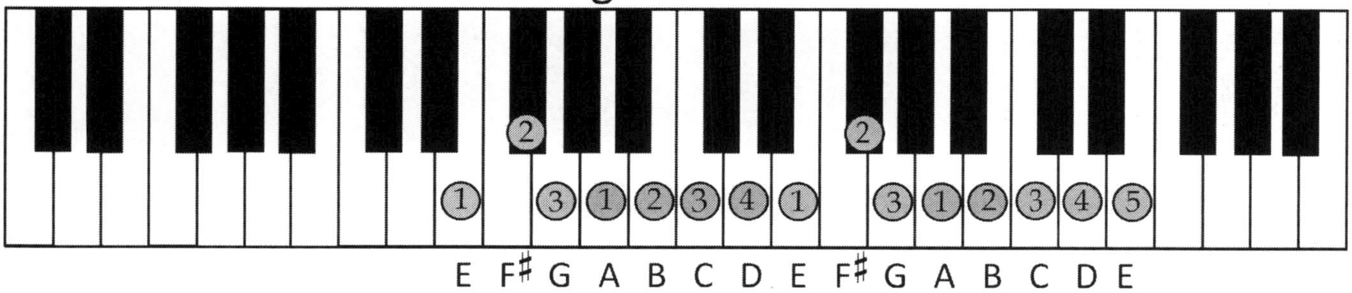

E natural minor scale - left hand

OR

Left hand

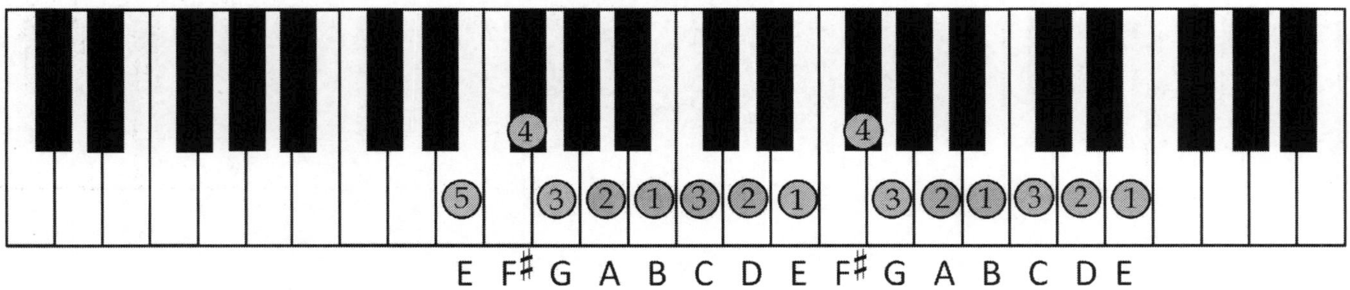

CHROMATIC SCALES

Chromatic scale starting on D - right hand

Chromatic scale starting on D - left hand

Right hand

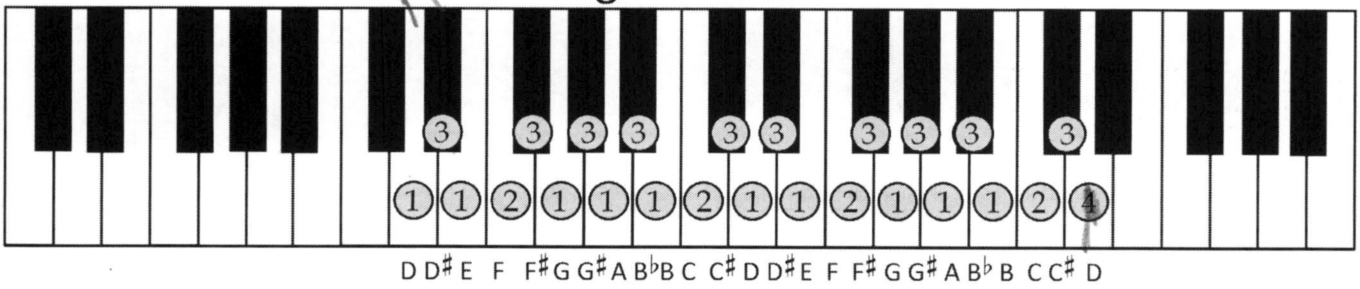

Left hand

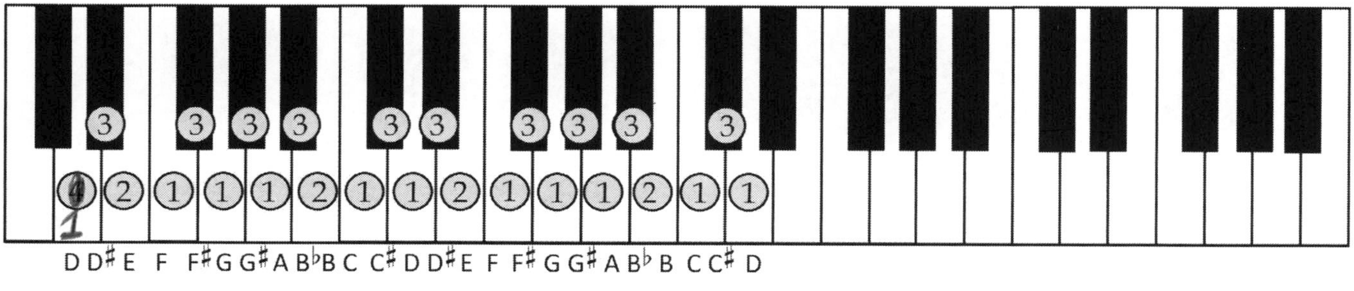

MAJOR BROKEN CHORDS

C major broken chord - right hand

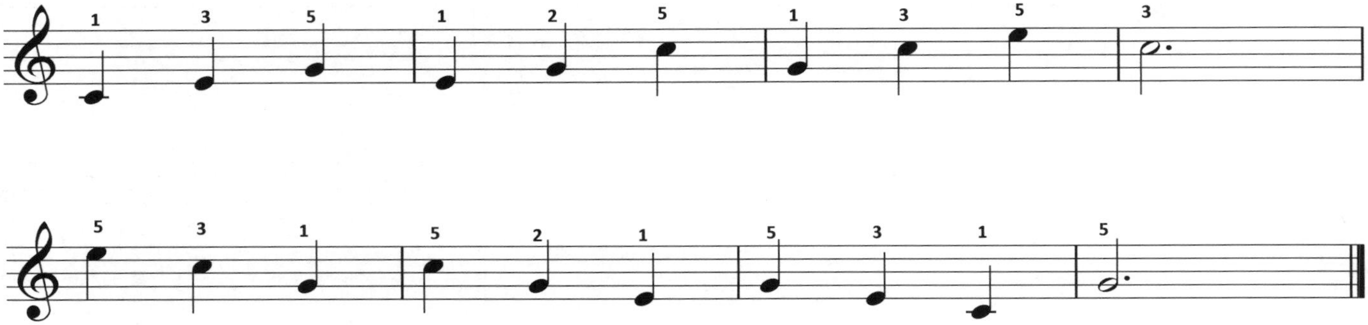

Right hand - ascending

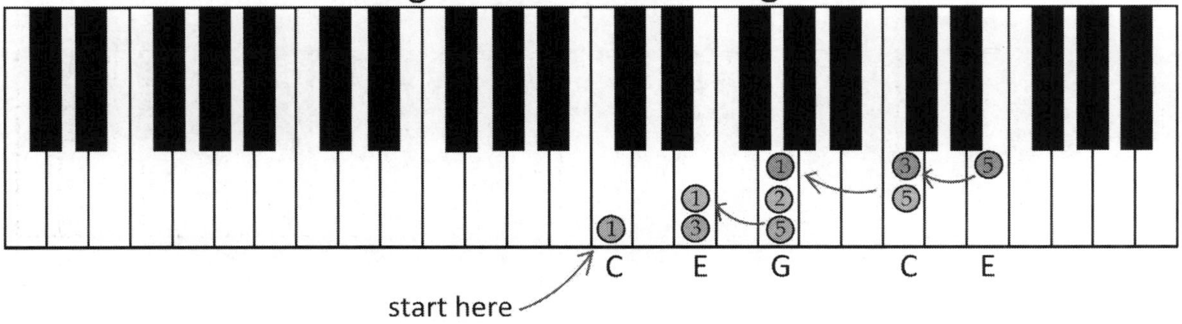

Right hand - descending

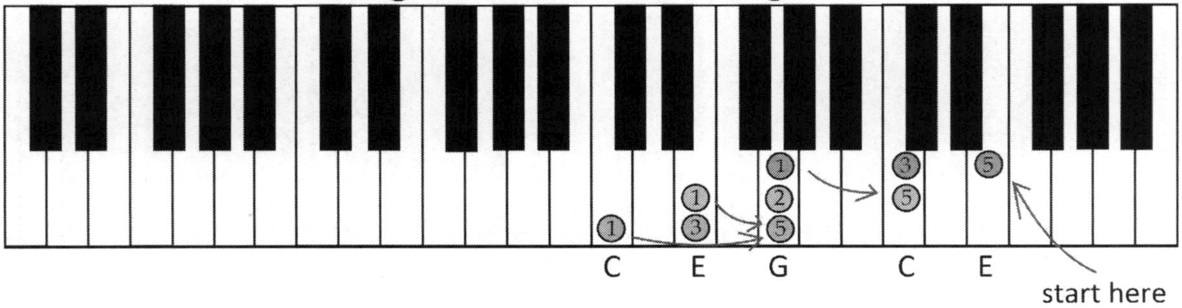

C major broken chord - left hand

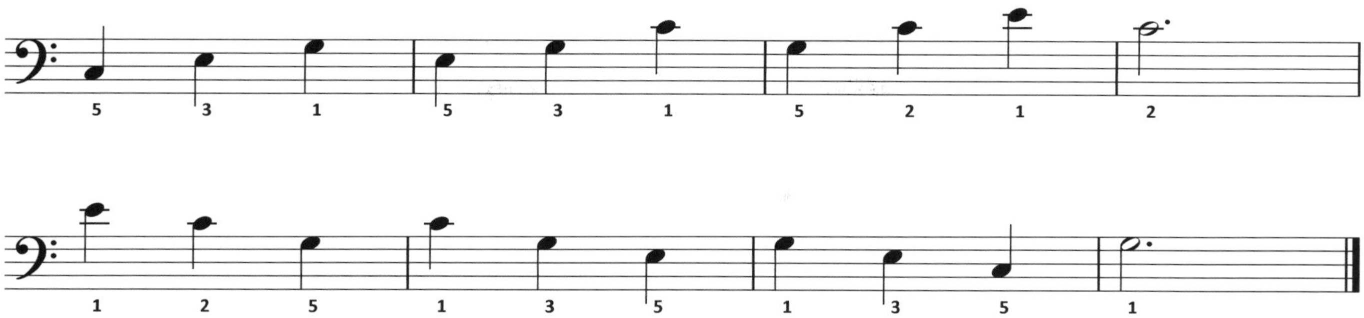

Left hand - ascending

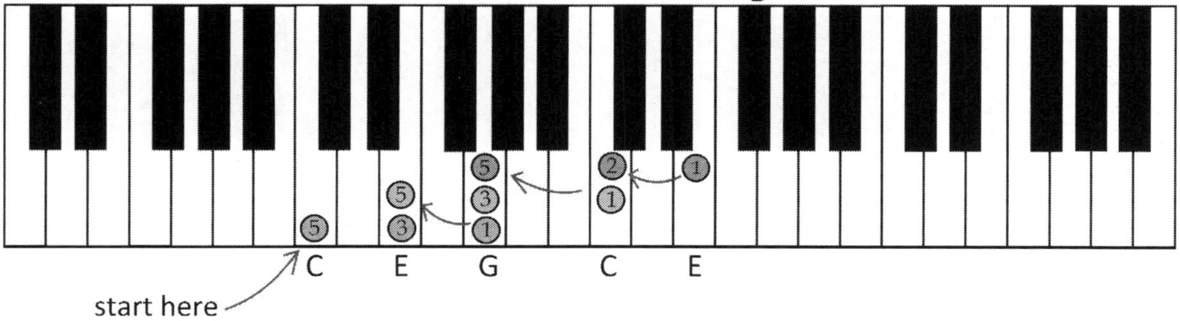

Left hand - descending

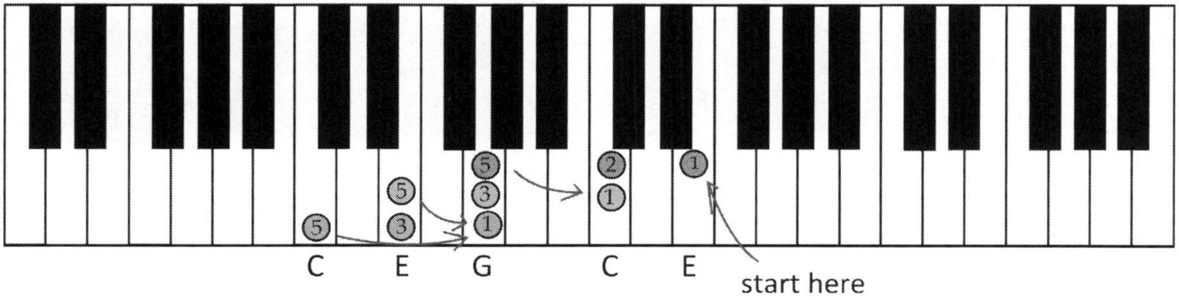

G major broken chord - right hand

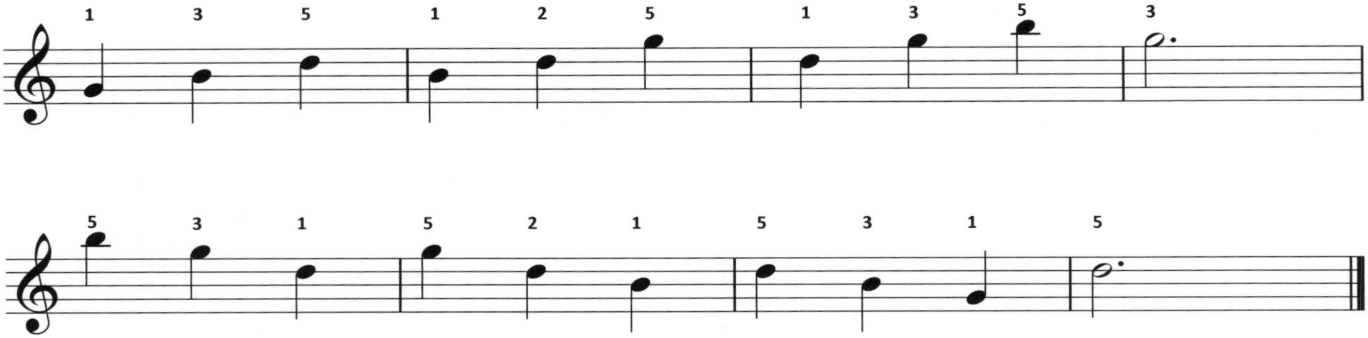

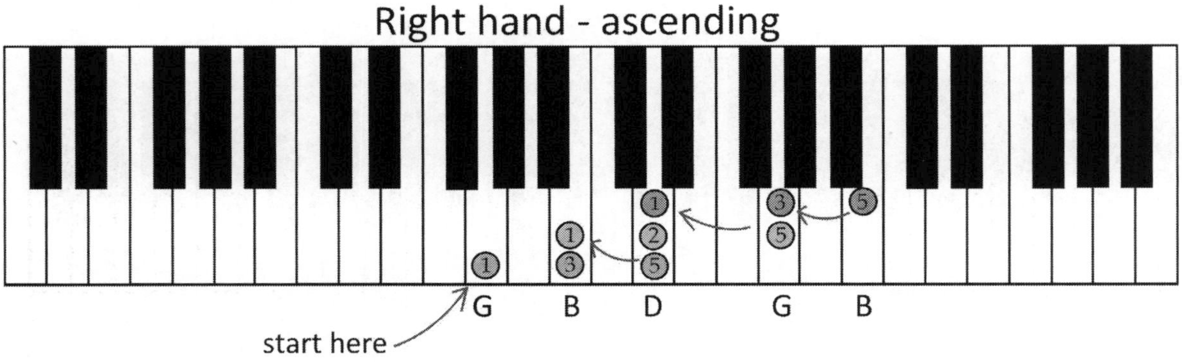

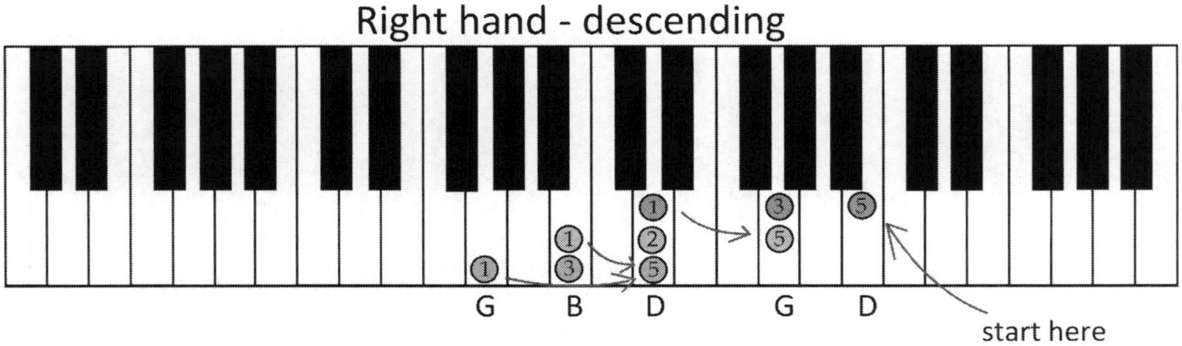

G major broken chord - left hand

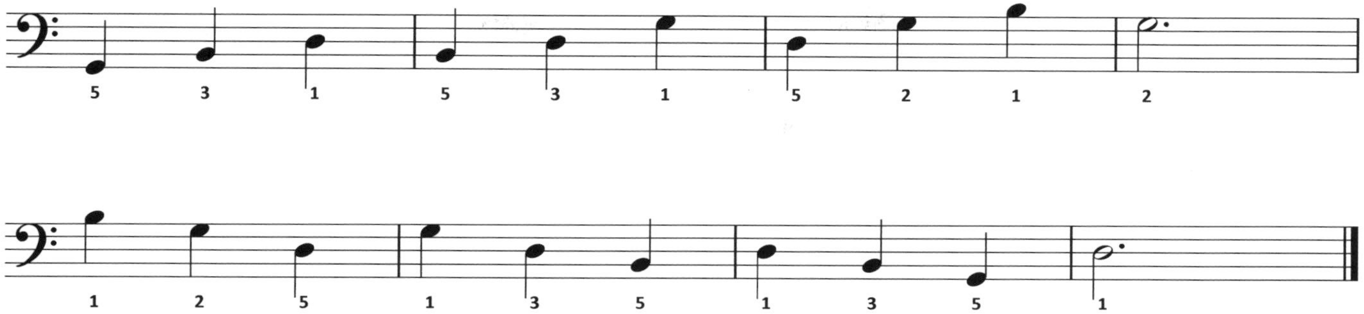

Left hand - ascending

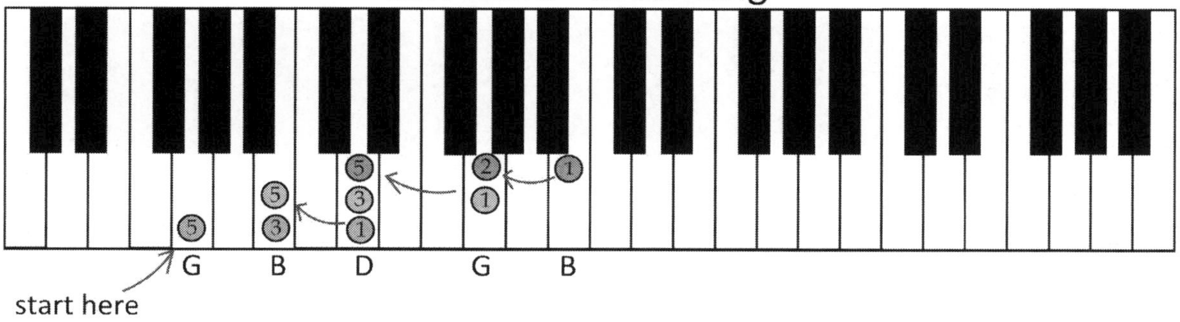

Left hand - descending

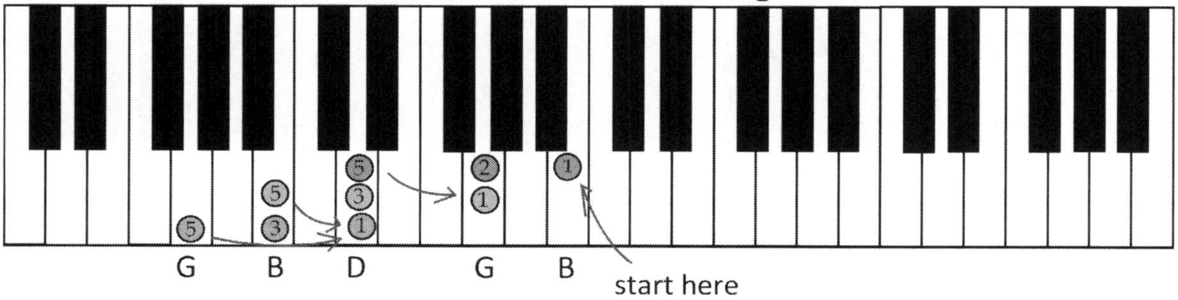

F major broken chord - right hand

Right hand - ascending

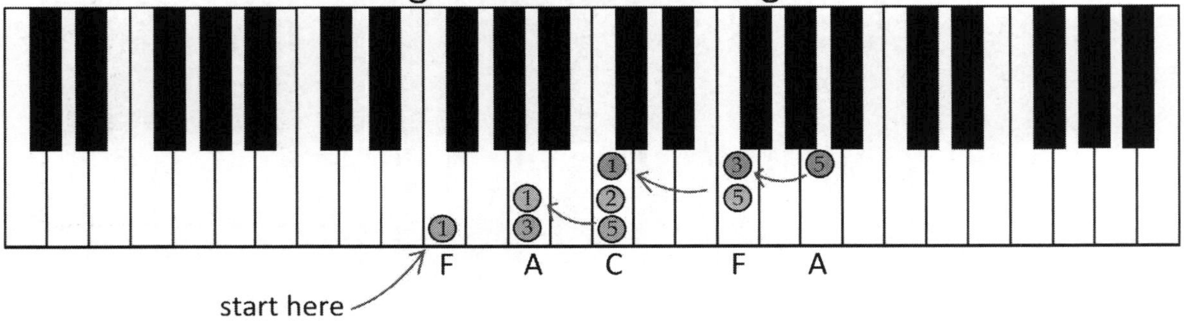

Right hand - descending

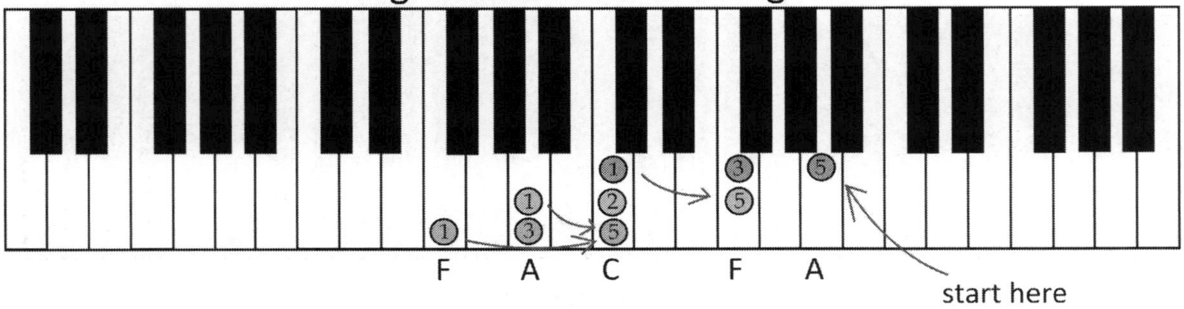

F major broken chord - left hand

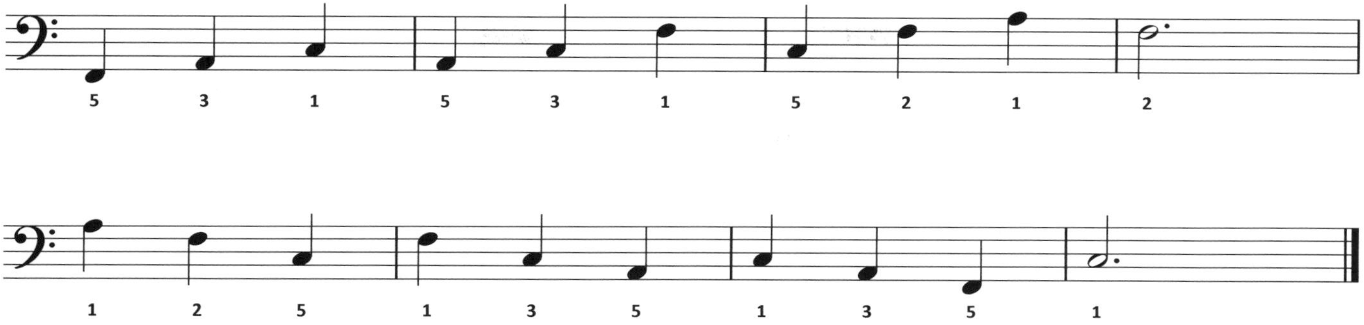

Left hand - ascending

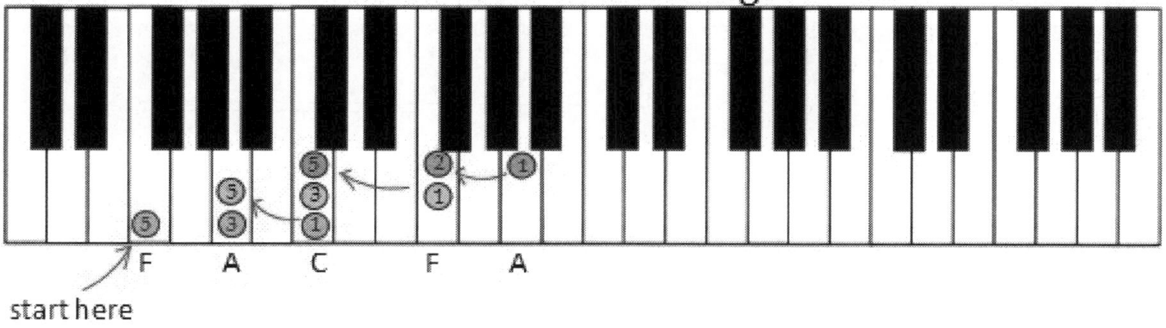

Left hand - descending

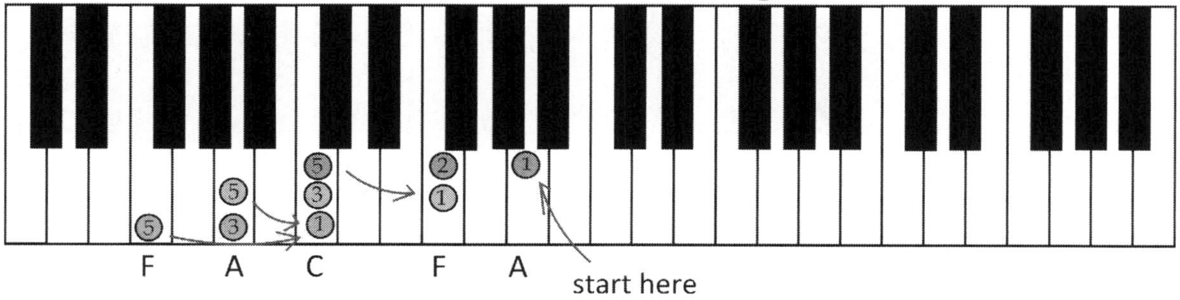

MINOR BROKEN CHORDS

D minor broken chord - right hand

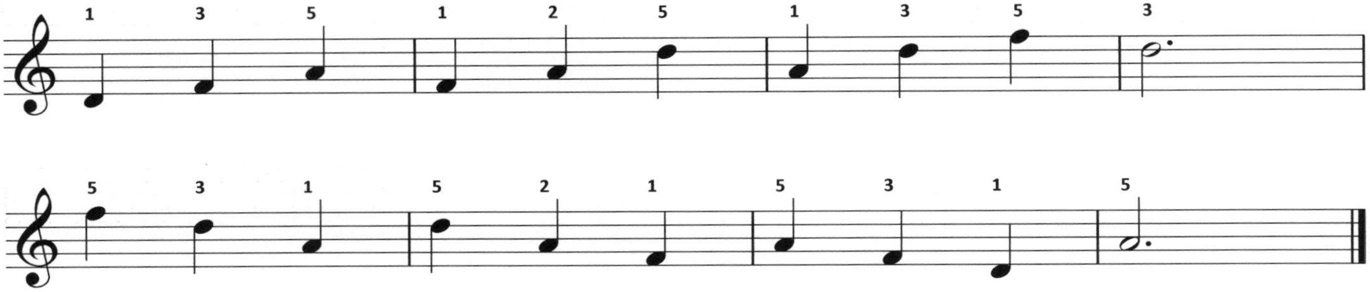

Right hand - ascending

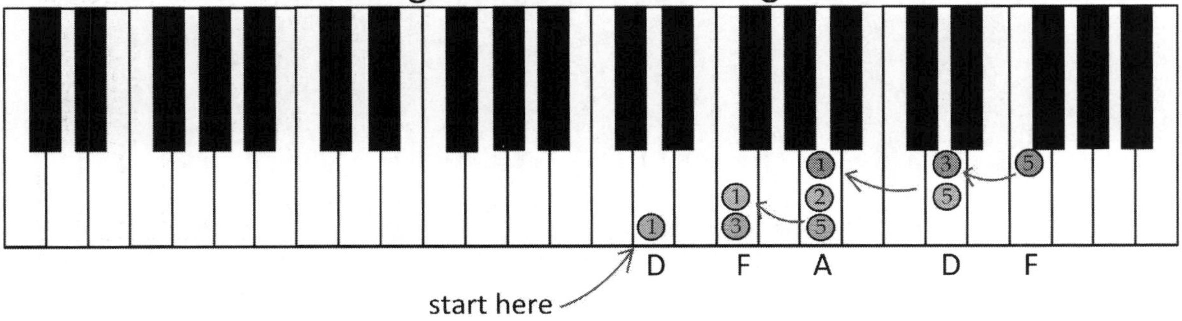

Right hand - descending

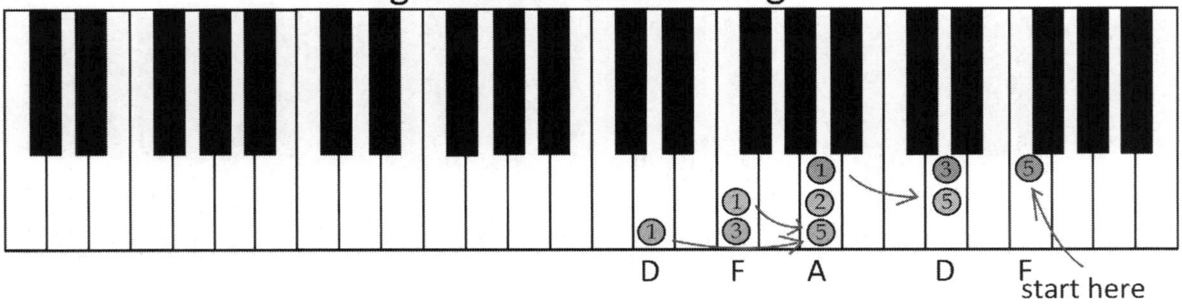

D minor broken chord - left hand

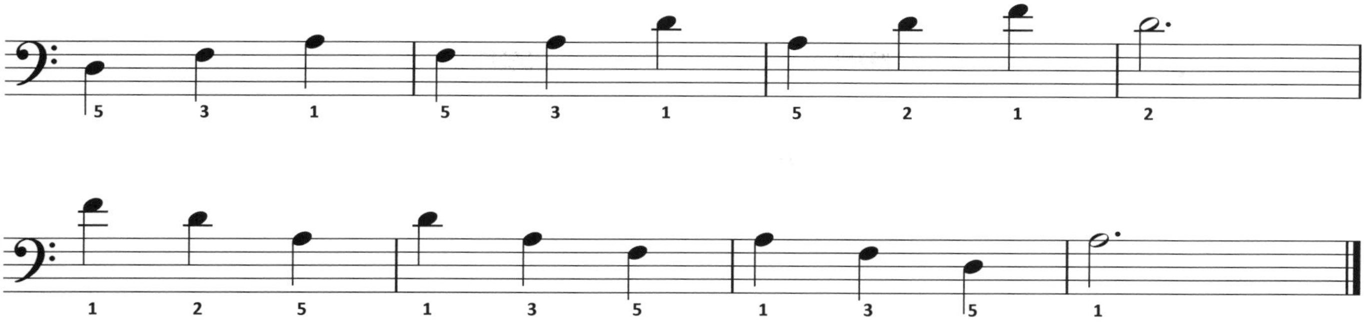

Left hand - ascending

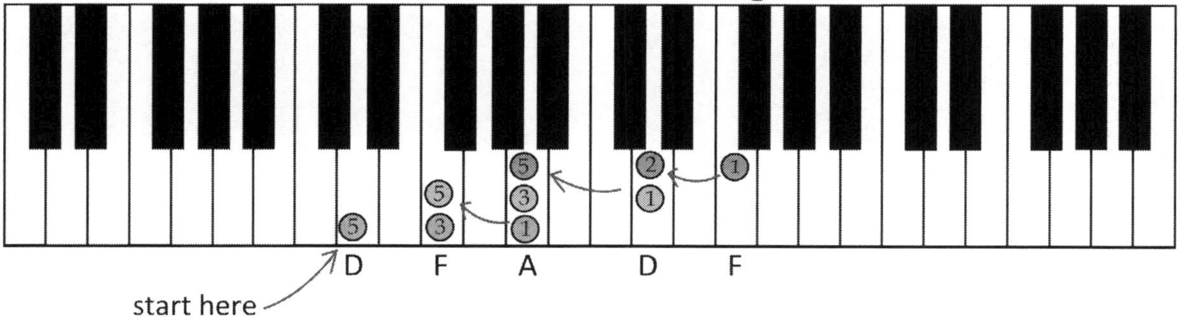

Left hand - descending

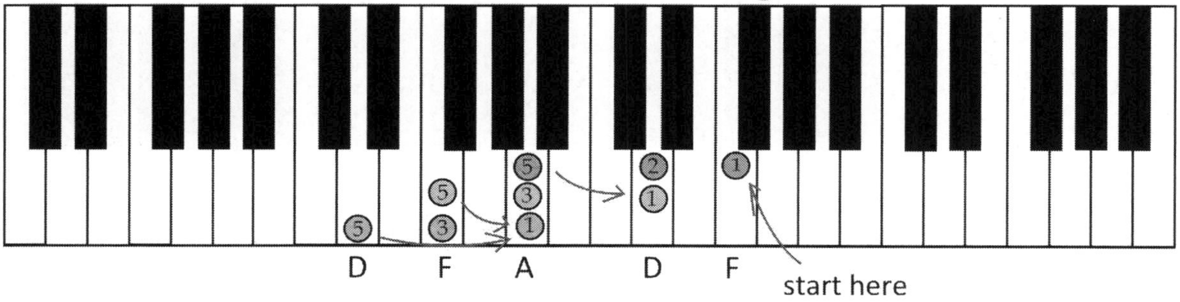

A minor broken chord - right hand

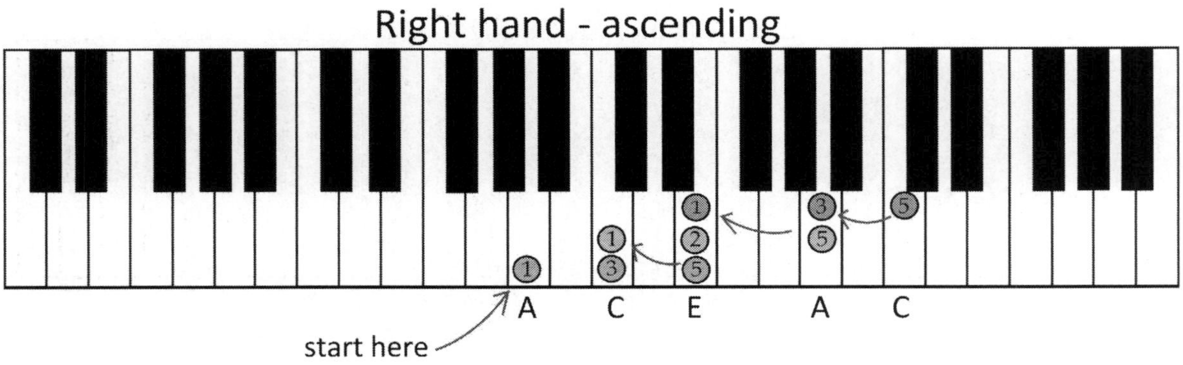

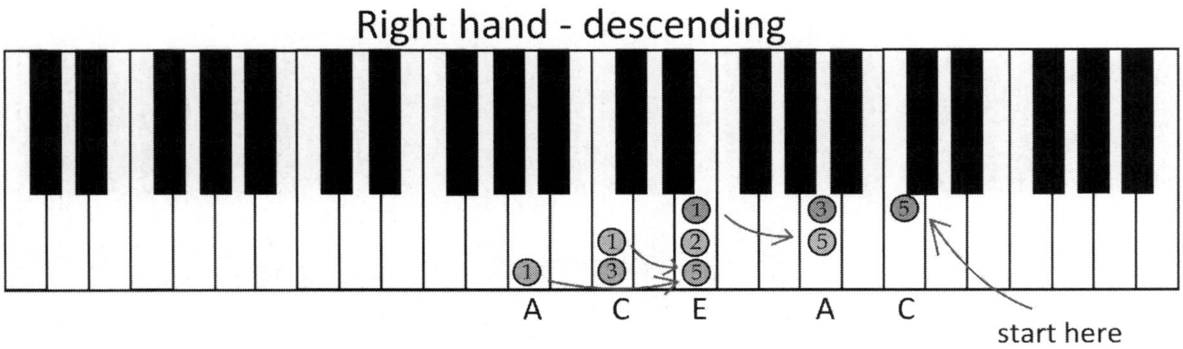

A minor broken chord - left hand

5 3 1 5 3 1 5 2 1 2

1 2 5 1 3 5 1 3 5 1

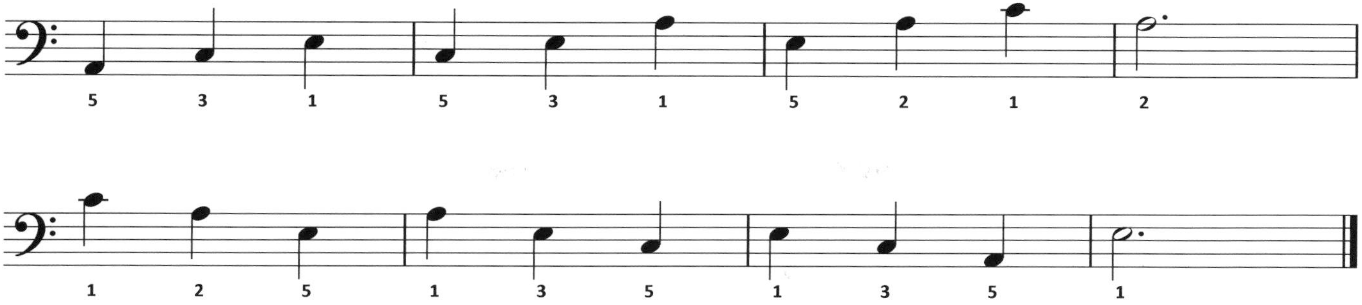

Left hand - ascending

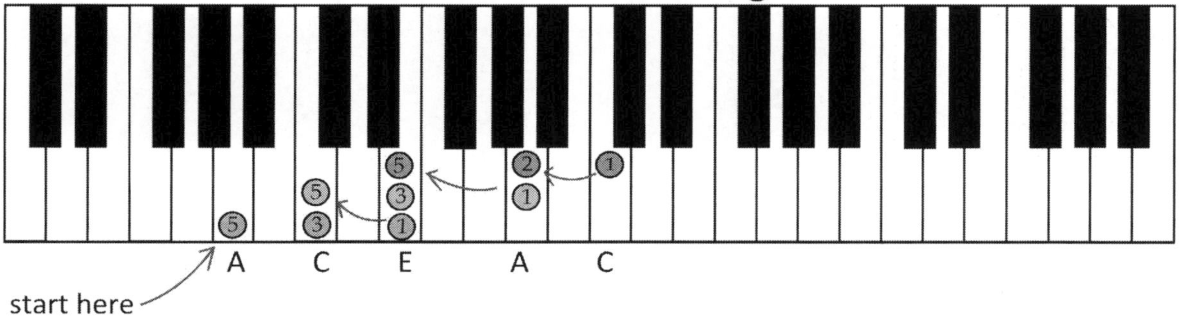

Left hand - descending

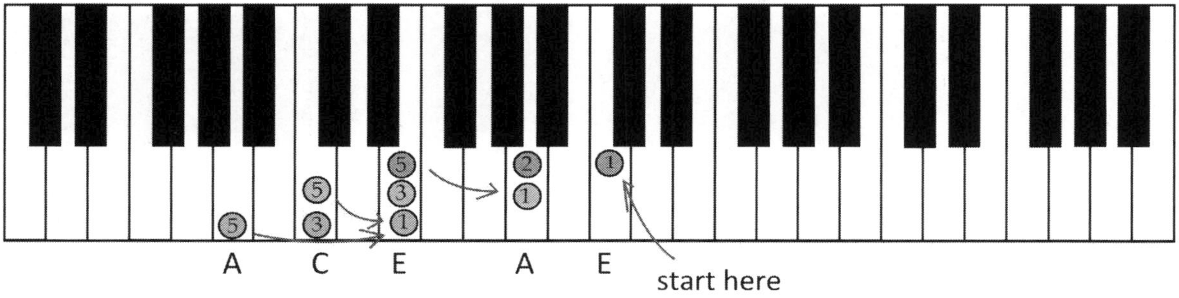

E minor broken chord - right hand

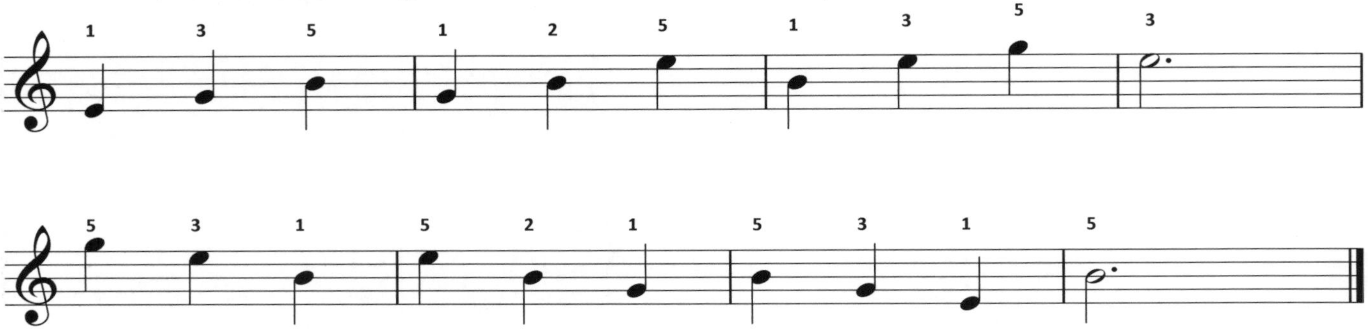

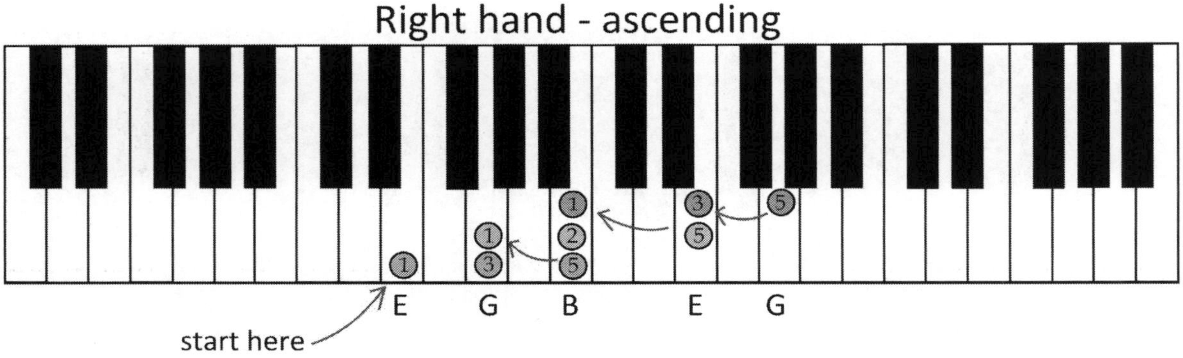

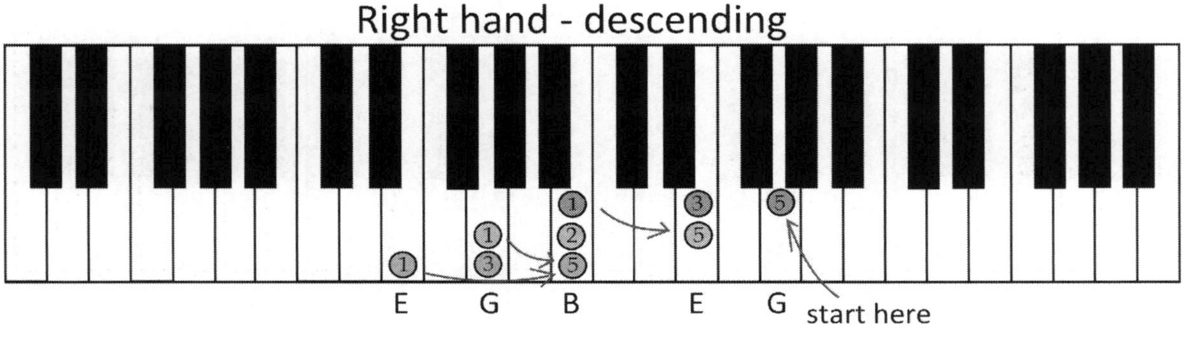

E minor broken chord - right hand

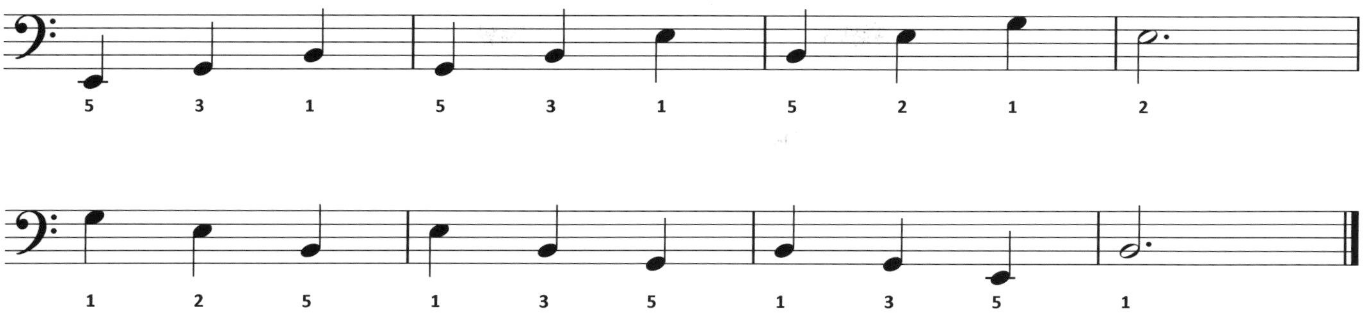

Left hand - ascending

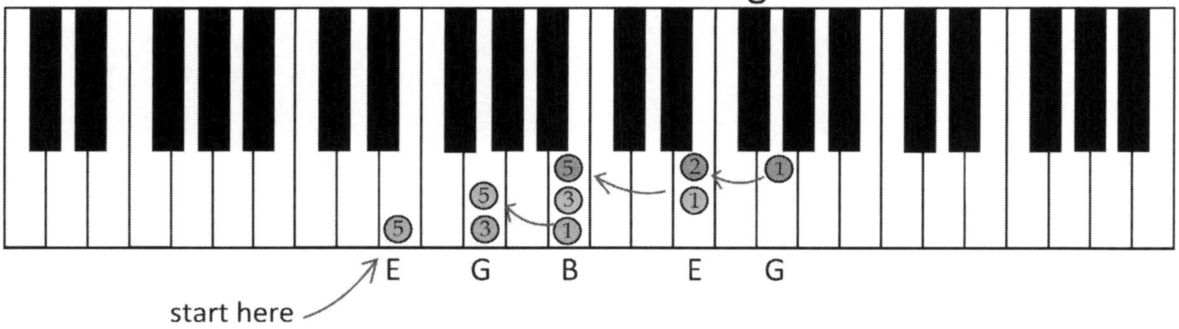

Left hand - descending

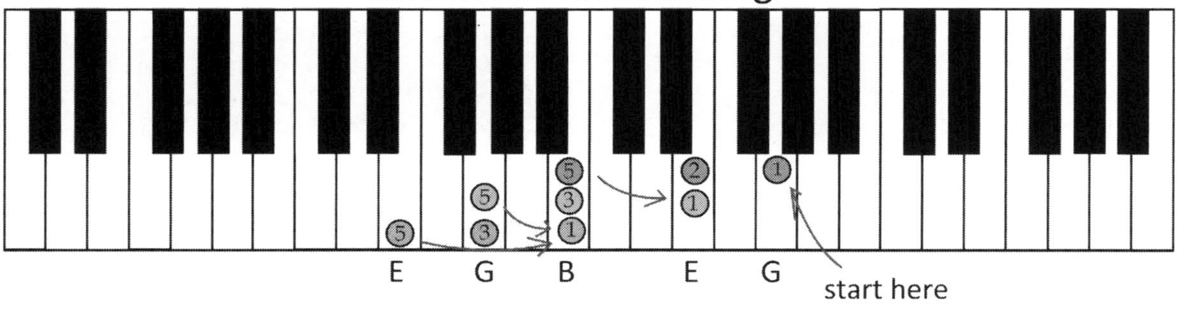

Progress Chart

Keep a record of which scales and broken chords you have learnt.

	Scales		Broken chords	
	Right hand	Left hand	Right hand	Left hand
C major				
G major				
D major				
F major				
A minor				
D minor				
E minor				
Chromatic scale				
C major - contrary motion				

18204543R00026

Printed in Great Britain
by Amazon